contents

- **6** Hello
- **8** Profile: Zalfie
- **10** The best subscriber milestone celebrations
- **12** Wordsearch
- **14** Pug cake
- **16** The rise of the Toy Vlogger
- **18** Profile: Toys AndMe
- **20** Spot the difference
- **22** Profile: Thatcher Joe
- **24** Vlogging all over the world
- **26** Profile: W2S
- **28** 5 epic YouTube things
- **30** Profile: JoJo Siwa
- **32** Say what?
- **34** Profile: Dan TDM
- **36** 5 favourite YouTube challenge videos
- **38** Profile: Mark Ferris

40 The beauty edit
42 Who is your vlogger BFF?
44 Profile: Ingrid Nilsen
46 5 awesome things we learned from Vsauce
48 Guess who?
50 My YouTube set
52 My YouTube channel
54 Profile: F2 Freestylers
56 Profile: Dan & Phil

58 The 7 second challenge
60 What type of YouTuber are you?
62 Top picks
64 Bestseller
66 Spot and find
68 14 times that YouTuber words inspired us
70 The ultimate vlogger quiz
74 Ones to watch
76 Answers

#Hello!

Welcome to the second edition of The Ultimate Guide to Vloggers.

You are in for a treat my friends! This issue is packed with all the goings-on from the wonderful world of YouTube, from what's trending to what's definitely not, and everything in between. Along with all the gossip from the YouTube family, we'll introduce you to some shiny new vloggers that are shaking things up for the better!

It's safe to say that YouTube stars are still on the rise with no sign of slowing down. Have you heard that "YouTuber" is now in the dictionary? It's totally true and we think it's about time, too.

Dictionary definition

A frequent user of the video-sharing website YouTube, especially someone who produces and appears in videos on the site.

TBH, we couldn't have put it better if we tried!

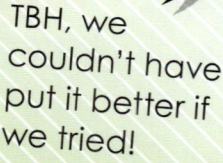

Zoella even got a mention in our all time fave soap, Coronation Street! Yes, you heard right and we are totes jealous.

YouTubers on the BIG SCREEN

Some of our beloved YouTubers were part of the Love Actually sequel in aid of Comic Relief. Alfie Deyes, Caspar Lee, Louise Pentland and Niomi Smart joined the all-star cast, including Hugh Grant and Martine McCutcheon 14 years after Love Actually was first released.

We love it when YouTubers do their bit for charity!

King of YOUTUBE

It's fair to say that PewDiePie can keep his YouTube crown, as he's STILL number 1. How does he do it?!

Worried you can't keep up with the vlogger lingo? Fear not, because we've got some handy phrases to get you started below. You can thank us later!

> **GRWM** – Get Ready With Me
> **AMA** – Ask Me Anything
> **AD** – This means that the video has been sponsored!
> **Haul** – A haul is when YouTubers talk you through all their fave buys from their shopping trip.
> **OOTD** – Outfit Of The Day – more of an Instagram kind of thing!
> **RN** – Right Now

It's time to catch up with everyone's FAVE YouTube couple, Zoella and Alfie! PLUS it's a good excuse to coo over their adorable pug, Nala (as if we needed one)!

If you don't already know, Zoe Sugg (aka Zoella) and Alfie Deyes are some of the best-loved and most successful vloggers on the planet! So you can only imagine how thrilled we were when they hooked up in 2014.

They live in Brighton together in a house that they've nicknamed the 'Zalfie Pad' that they share with their little pug, Nala. Both upload regular videos for their ginormous fan-bases and are doing a pretty good job of taking over the world with their YouTube success stories.

Zalfie

Zalfie moments we're obsessed with:

There's never a dull moment when you're around these guys. Check out this yoga challenge video, but be warned, we suspect you'll have serious workout gear envy when you see what Alfie surprises Zoe with. We sure did!

CHECK IT OUT

Zoella and Alfie often hang out with Alfie's sister, Poppy. She's a blogger with a whopping social media following of her own. Poppy dates a YouTuber called Sean Elliott O'Connor.

What's new?

Both Zoella and Alfie's channels continue to grow in popularity. Zoella's subscriber count reached a massive 11,674,680, and Alfie's PointlessBlog has 5,540,466 subscribers!
#powercouple

Zalfie are real life besties with Janya (Tanya Burr and Jim Chapman, incase you were wondering!) and we LOVE it when they all collaborate.

What we can't get enough of...

The fact that Zoella was mentioned on the nation's fave soap of all time, Coronation Street!
#winning

Guess what...

Zoe is 3 ½ years older than Alfie!

Zoe's 27th Birthday cake in the shape of a unicorn was pretty much the best thing we've ever seen.

Not many couples would be brave enough to take a lie detector test to share with the world - scrap that, not many couples would be brave enough to take one, full stop. But Zalfie would, and that's what makes Zoe and Alfie legit the coolest couple we know.

CHECK IT OUT

the best subscriber milestone

Your channel hits 1 million subscribers, but how would you mark the occasion? Here's our top 6 ways that YouTubers have celebrated hitting landmark numbers of subscribers!

CHECK IT OUT

Zoella...

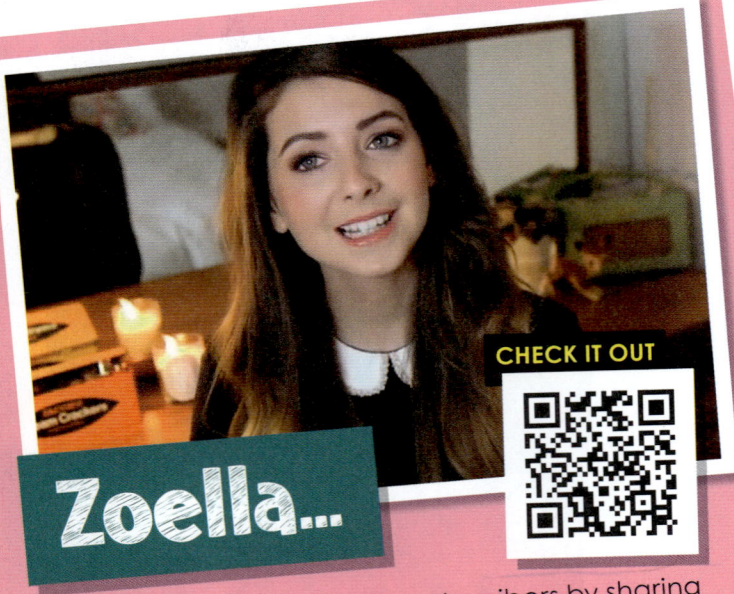

celebrated hitting 4 million subscribers by sharing a home video of her first and never-before-seen vlog, aged just 11 years old. D'awww... cute! We're still trying to figure out how young Zoe knew what vlogging was before it was even invented. One thing's for sure - she was a total natural, even back then! No wonder this gal's queen of the internet!

Caspar Lee...

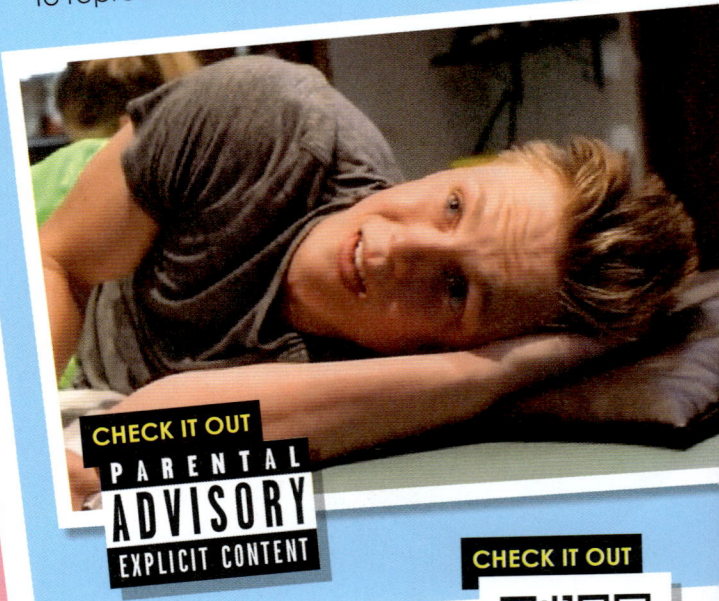

celebrated reaching a whopping 7 million subscribers by getting a teeny tiny triangle tattoo on his ankle. "But why a triangle?" I hear you ask! Well, to represent the YouTube "play button" of course.

CHECK IT OUT

PARENTAL ADVISORY EXPLICIT CONTENT

CHECK IT OUT

Thatcher Joe

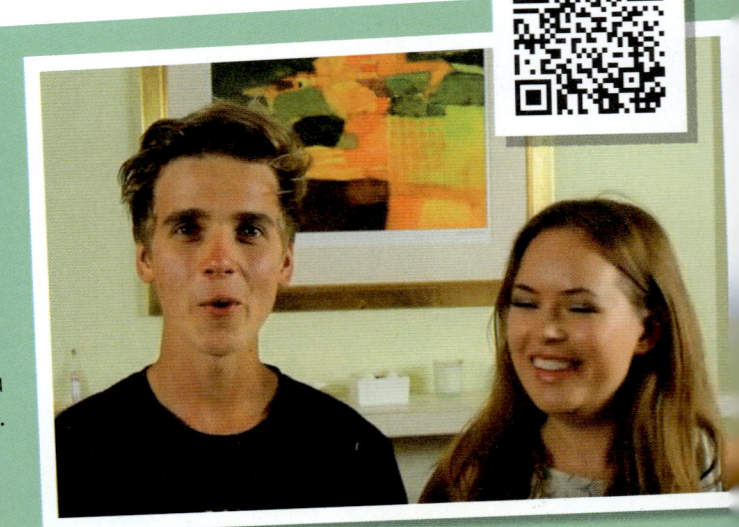

When Thatcher Joe hit 500,000 subscribers (which was quite some time ago!), he threw a YouTube party for all his vlogger pals. As you'd expect, it wasn't just a casual get together, oh no. In true Joe Sugg style, his party was packed with some good old-fashioned party games and a generous helping of challenges from the likes of Tanya Burr.

celebrations

Tom Cassell

The Syndicate Project's Tom Cassell chose to skydive when he reached a milestone 1,000,000 subscribers. He even dragged along his Dad and his godfather to throw themselves out of the plane, too. So, just your average day then, really!

CHECK IT OUT

Toys AndMe

Tiana from Toys AndMe happened to be boarding a swanky flight to New York when she discovered her channel reached 4 million subscribers! Talk about living the high life! #LifeGoals

CHECK IT OUT

Mark Ferris

CHECK IT OUT

When Mark Ferris reached 10,000 subscribers he asked his viewers to tweet him one word that sums up his channel. He wrote the fan's name and their word on balloons, before releasing them up into the sky. If that wasn't enough cuteness for one video, he also included lots of highlight clips of his best bits! So cute, we want to watch it again!

How YOU would celebrate a landmark number of subscribers?
On a blank piece of paper, write down how you would celebrate.

#WORDSEARCH

On your marks, get set, SEARCH! Can you spot all of the Vlogger channels sneakily hidden in this big grid? Cross them off as you find them.

- MOREZOELLA
- POINTLESS
- EVERYDAYJIM
- MARCUSBUTLERTV
- JENNAMARBLES
- INGRIDNILSEN
- JIMCHAPMAN
- FAMTASTIC
- JOJOVLOGS
- DANTDM
- RYANTOYSREVIEW
- EXTRATYLER
- INTHEFROW
- FABULOUSHANNAH
- MARKFERRIS

X	Q	S	S	B	G	W	K	R	S	M	F	C	V	G	Z	J	O	E	A
N	A	O	O	A	P	K	Z	I	V	A	D	T	A	W	X	E	I	I	G
X	U	L	A	F	Z	Y	R	R	M	D	R	P	X	K	I	N	H	N	G
L	M	G	L	K	B	R	M	T	E	E	I	L	F	N	U	N	A	T	A
T	H	F	Y	E	E	X	A	D	L	P	G	Z	J	N	F	A	H	H	L
K	W	S	A	F	O	S	R	T	C	T	O	W	M	I	G	M	A	E	H
C	U	I	K	B	T	Z	U	B	E	K	X	T	E	J	N	A	X	F	L
Z	P	R	D	I	U	B	E	M	A	F	G	G	N	K	E	R	H	R	X
N	A	X	C	C	S	L	V	R	Y	H	J	C	I	T	K	B	O	O	S
M	U	F	M	U	C	F	O	P	O	X	L	N	N	O	L	L	H	W	P
M	M	Y	C	V	H	R	O	U	N	M	G	U	Q	U	U	E	G	R	K
Z	D	R	Y	A	N	T	O	Y	S	R	E	V	I	E	W	S	S	X	K
L	A	T	L	Y	E	P	T	C	I	H	A	R	A	B	R	H	R	S	W
M	R	U	N	C	Z	W	V	D	V	T	A	Z	M	X	J	Q	E	D	H
T	N	X	G	A	J	J	N	I	X	N	R	N	I	P	U	A	L	Z	R
S	F	D	N	R	D	I	F	U	T	G	R	D	N	Y	O	N	Y	J	B
A	X	S	C	O	L	V	O	J	O	J	F	U	G	A	L	Q	T	H	Q
S	L	C	Q	S	Q	G	F	Y	C	F	S	Q	U	X	H	J	A	P	F
W	F	E	E	N	H	D	W	Z	D	Y	U	Q	I	K	U	X	R	F	W
D	V	N	N	V	Q	M	I	J	Y	A	D	Y	R	E	V	E	T	J	F
B	K	Z	U	O	P	K	T	H	W	T	N	P	G	Y	I	K	X	J	C
M	H	V	N	Y	Y	Y	W	R	B	Y	C	Q	P	P	V	M	X	E	G	L
I	P	Q	X	G	G	J	I	M	C	H	A	P	M	A	N	S	T	R	J

Check your anwers on page 76

BAKING pug cookies

If you love pugs as much as we do, you'll be sure to adore this dreamy recipe! Get your arty hat on for some serious icing.

For the biscuits, you'll need:
250g butter
140g caster sugar
1 egg yolk
2tsp vanilla essence
320g plain flour
Colourful icing pens! We chose black and red.

(Makes around 20 using 7cm cookie cutters)

1. Mix together the butter and sugar in a large mixing bowl.

2. Add the egg yolk and stir together.

3. Then, mix in the flour.

4. Now you're ready to roll out your cookie dough. First, dust some more flour onto a flat surface, adding a sprinkle more flour if it's still a bit sticky. Roll out using a rolling pin until the dough is roughly ½ centimetre thin.

5 Use round cookie cutters to cut out lots of circle shapes and pop onto a baking tray lined with greaseproof paper.

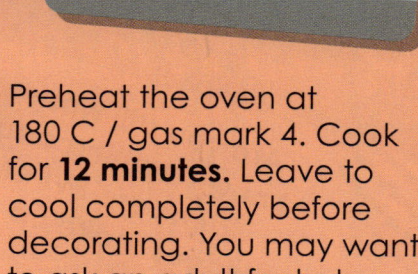

6 Preheat the oven at 180 C / gas mark 4. Cook for **12 minutes**. Leave to cool completely before decorating. You may want to ask an adult for help.

to decorate

1 Draw 2 round eyes.

2 Now draw an upside down sausage shape underneath the eyes, like this.

3 Draw 2 triangles for the cute pug ears!

TOP TIP!
If you don't fancy baking, you could just decorate some ready-made biscuits!

4 When the icing has set, add a cheeky little red tongue.

The rise of the toy vlogger

All there is to know about the rise of toy vlogging and the unboxing phenomena!

Are you still wondering what unboxing vlogs are? If you know anything about YouTube, you'll know that unboxing videos are EVERYWHERE RN. Toy reviews and unboxing videos make up one of the biggest genres on YouTube.

Major toy brands (we're talking as big as Lego and Disney) rely on popular vloggers to feature their latest toys on their channels. It's a way for subscribers to find out what's brand new and what toys are the most fun. The more subscribers a vlogger has, the more likely they are to be sent lots of cool toys to review and play with.

But what exactly do toy vloggers do?

CHECK IT OUT

Think of them like reviewers or toy testers (I know, life goals or what?!). Vloggers are filmed playing with the toys and talking about what the toy can do as well as what they love or dislike about it. Some of the most viewed toy vlogs are when they use the toys for fun family challenges or silly stunts. Check out this "Giant Donut vs Giant Pizza!" challenge from Toys AndMe.

surprise UNBOXING

One of the most popular types of toy vlogs is the surprise unboxing videos. Surprise unboxing is really popular with collectible toys such as L.O.L. Surprise Dolls or Lego, where the vlogger doesn't know what's inside until they open it on camera.

Check out these popular toy vloggers:

Ryan Toys Review

Ryan ToysReview is a US-based toy vlogger with a hugely successful channel of toy reviews for kids by a kid. Ryan loves everything from trains to superheroes and since his channel launched in March 2015, he's already earned himself 6,886,969 subscribers. Not bad, Ryan!

Kiddie Toys Review

Kiddie Toys Review is Ely and Ela's toy channel where they unbox giant surprise packages and review Hello Kitty, Frozen, Doc McStuffins and many, many more!

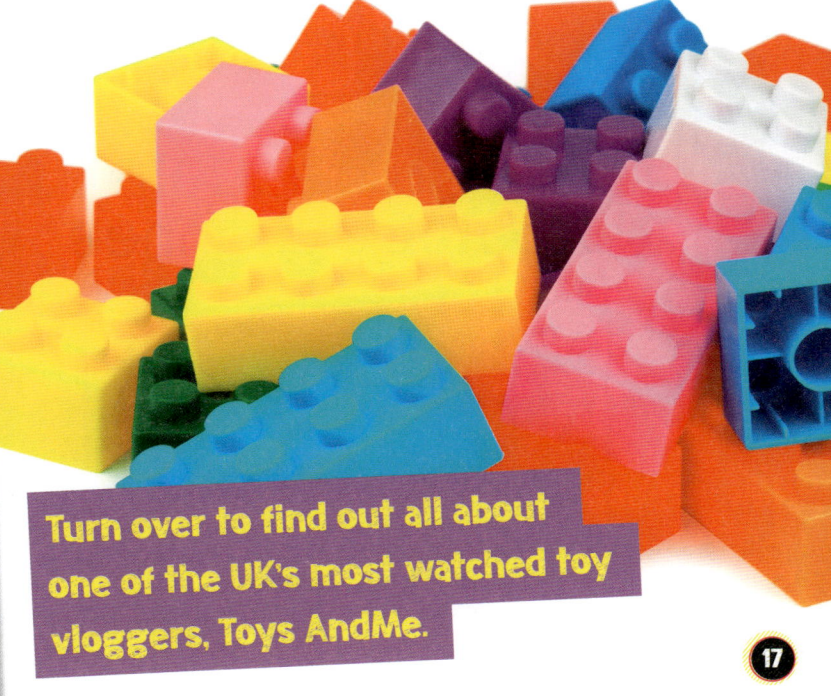

Turn over to find out all about one of the UK's most watched toy vloggers, Toys AndMe.

toys andme

▶ YouTube channels

First channel - Toys AndMe This is Tiana's main channel where she opens and reviews awesome toys and candy, as well as taking part in LOL challenges.

Newer channel - Famtastic A space for more fun with Tiana and all her family – from travel vlogs, more gross challenges and more toys!

Name: Tiana
DOB: 24/08/2007
Siblings: A big brother called Jordan
Likes: Collecting Shopkins
Dislikes: BBQ sauce – eww!

 @toys_andme

bio

Tiana aka TT is a British vlogger famous for her toy-based YouTube channel, Toys AndMe. This super fun channel is packed with toy and candy reviews, unboxing videos, as well as wacky challenges featuring her Mum, Dad, brother and of course, her BFFs!

Inspired by other young YouTubers reviewing toys, Tiana asked her parents if she could do the same. In April 2015, Tiana (with the help of her Dad) uploaded her very first video called "New Kids Toy Channel" and the rest is history! It wasn't long before Tiana built up a loyal fan base, reaching over 4.4 million subscribers to her YouTube channel, aged 9. Pretty impressive!

Massive toy brands such as Shopkins, Barbie and Minecraft send their latest toys to Tiana just so that she can vlog about them! Tiana's a natural in front of the camera and full of enthusiasm when she's doing her surprise unboxing videos or just chatting to her many, many loyal fans! Her fans mean everything to Tiana and she makes lots of time for Q+As and fan mail videos, too.

3 of the best

Stuck Inside Giant Balloons Challenge

CHECK IT OUT

Power Wheels Ride On Car Funny Fails!

CHECK IT OUT

Ball Pit Challenge In My House

CHECK IT OUT

TOY STORE LOCK IN

Tiana once stayed in a toystore overnight! She really is too cool.

#SPOT THE diffrence

D'aww! Look who it is. But wait a sec... looks like something fishy has been going on in the pictures below. Can you spot all 8 differences between pictures A and picture B?

Check your anwers on page 76

thatcher joe
aka Joe Sugg

> "I didn't choose the Sugg life, the Sugg life chose me."

DOB: 08/09/1991

Siblings: Zoe Sugg – you may have heard of her…?

Pets: No, but he gets to hang out with Zoella's pug a lot. That counts, right?

Likes: Skateboarding

Dislikes: Rollercoasters

- @ThatcherJoe
- @joe_sugg
- @Joe_Sugg

YouTube channels

ThatcherJoe – Joe's main channel with 7,851,256 subscribers.

ThatcherJoeVlogs – This is a place to share all the things that Joe gets up to on his days off.

ThatcherJoeGames – Playthroughs, reviews and challenge me videos!

bio

If you're looking for a channel filled with pranks, challenges and hilarious impressions, Joe Sugg is the answer to all your prayers. British vlogger, Joe Sugg is Zoella's younger brother, but he's so much more than just Zoe's kid brother. I think his Sugglets would vouch for the fact that he's found his feet in the world of YouTube.

You may know this YouTuber by his nickname, Thatcher Joe, and that's because young Joe spent his early career thatching people's roofs. He started vlogging in 2011 and is now thought of as one of the most successful YouTubers of our time, as well as being a successful author with his own book series to boot.

Whether he's filling his housemates room with hundreds of cups of water, filling the bathroom with mousetraps (do not try this at home!), or just peg pranking his sister Zoe – you can never predict what this guy will think up next. And it's all in the name of entertaining his loyal subscribers who he likes to call "Sugglets".

3 of the best

Most viewed!

CHECK IT OUT

My Sister Does My Make-up has over 17 million views!

Collab!

CHECK IT OUT

Singing Impressions With Conor Maynard

True talent

CHECK IT OUT

Joe's incredible skill for doing spot on impressions has set him apart from any competition. Watch some of them here. You can thank us later!

JOE'S AN AUTHOR

He's got a series of books: Username Evie, Username Regenerated, Username Uprising.

HIS BFF

Caspar Lee!! This fun loving pair used to be housemates and they've even starred in a movie together, Joe and Caspar Hit the Road. Make sure you check this out, if you haven't already that is!

Vlogging all over the world

We all know our Zoella Sugg from our Tanya Burr, but do YOU know who's who in the big old world beyond the UK? Passports at the ready everyone - it's time to check out the YouTube talent from across the globe.

America

Bethany Mota is basically America's answer to Zoella. She began vlogging in 2009 on her YouTube channel "Macbarbie07" and rose to fame for her fashion hauls. These days her lifestyle channel is packed with everything from daily routines, comedy, cooking, beauty, DIYs and travel. She's even got her own clothing line at Aéropostale.

Subscribers: 10 million+

Spain

Ruben Doblas Gundersen, better known on YouTube as El Rubius is best known for his gameplays and vlogs, which include walkthroughs, challenges, sketches and reviews. He has two channels, "elrubius" and "elrubiusOMG" and he's the most followed Spanish YouTube star. If that wasn't enough, he also has a bestselling book called "Troll".

2.5 billion total views and 13.6 million total subscribers

Sweden

Subscribers: 54,522,998

Yup, you've guessed it... **PewDiePie**. Felix Kjellberg has been vlogging since 2010 and is best known for his gaming videos! His amazing pet pugs Edgar and Maya also have a big following, and when you see their faces it's clear why they're such a hit. His fans, or "Bro Army" as Felix refers to them, just can't get enough of his content and PewDiePie just keeps on delivering!

Mexico

Yuya, aka Mariand Castrejon, is Mexico's go-to beauty vlogger and YouTuber. She decided to start up her YouTube channel aged 16 after winning a make-up contest. Since then, her subscribers grew and grew, to the enormous following that she's built today. In 2016, Yuya joined the United Nations' Sustainable Development Action Campaign, fighting for gender equality and to empower women and girls.

Subscribers: 17,984,479

Australia

Subscribers: 362,190

Meet Aussie YouTube star, **Sammy Robinson**. Her beauty and fashion filled channel is a mix of hair and make-up tutorials, fashion hauls, challenges and GRWM videos, which she uploads twice a week. We especially love her celebrity inspired make-up tutorials, as well as any that involve her travels to exotic destinations! Take us with you next time, Sammy. Cheers!

W2S
aka WROETOSHAW

Name: Harry Lewis
DOB: 24/11/1996
Siblings: Younger brother Josh and younger sister Rosie.

@W2S
@wroetoshaw
@wroetoshaw

▶ YouTube channels

@W2S – This is where you'll find your challenges and dares aplenty!
@W2Splays – A channel dedicated to playing random games. Enjoy!

> One of the biggest FIFA vloggers on YouTube

bio

Harry's originally from the island of Guernsey, but has since moved to London, living the true YouTuber dream. Harry's flatmates are also YouTubers, and they're called Callux and Calfreezy #SquadGoals! Harry is a YouTube gameplay commentator who primarily posts FIFA gameplay footage as well as live commentary videos, as he plays.

As well as gaming, Harry also films heaps of extreme challenge videos, which are (unsurprisingly) very popular too! Highlights from his super high-energy videos include everything from extreme garden football to giant football slip 'n' slide with his Mum, and trampoline challenges (don't try ANY of these at home!). One thing's for sure, there's never a dull moment over on W2S. I mean, geez, wait up while we catch our breath. What makes these videos extra special is the way that he ropes in brave family members or daring pals - rather them than us...

And he's a generous fella, too. Harry once sent £50 to each of his followers who received straight A* and A's at GCSE. All his followers needed to do was tweet him proof of their grades!

FUN FACT!
Harry's become well known for his trademark blue jumper.

3 of the best

Greatest FIFA pack opening of all time!

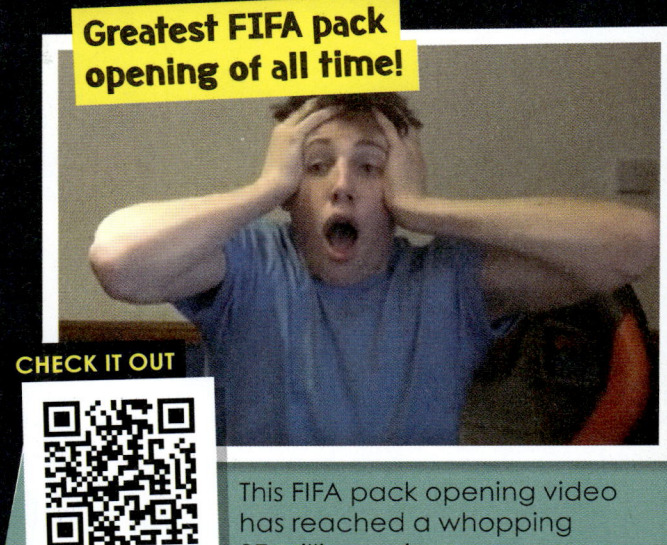

CHECK IT OUT

This FIFA pack opening video has reached a whopping 37 million + views.

Top 10 W2S Moments

CHECK IT OUT

Sidemen Crossbar Challenge

CHECK IT OUT

5 epic YouTube things

YouTubers always have THE most fun and if you're anything like us, sometimes you wish you could have just one day in their life. These are our top picks of the things we wish we'd thought of first.

1 MAKING A BALL PIT IN OUR HOUSE

The video involving Alfie Deyes transforming his house into a ball pit is too much to deal with. What else would you do when your girlfriend's away? You have to see it to believe it.

CHECK IT OUT

2 ULTIMATE ROOM MAKEOVER PRANK

Oli White's Ultimate Room Makeover may have been a big effort, but the result was totally worth it. Just over 200 posters and a couple of hours' later, Oli's birthday surprise for his brother was definitely a memorable one.

CHECK IT OUT

PARENTAL ADVISORY EXPLICIT CONTENT

BAD KIDS DRIVING POWER WHEELS RIDE ON CAR - MCDONALDS DRIVE THRU PRANK!

We'll never get over the time that Tiana from Toys AndMe went to McDonald's drive through in a toy car and used the actual drive through! That's one way to deal with your parents burning the dinner.

4 ULTIMATE BALLOON PRANK ON MY ROOMMATE

The result of Joe Sugg's balloon prank on Caspar Lee was nothing short of spectacular. Caspar's room was so full of colourful balloons that it was fit to burst. We thought it couldn't get any better... and then Oli White appeared from amongst the balloons to surprise him. We wish we could have been there to witness all the excitement! Major FOMO.

CHECK IT OUT

5 DO THE MIRANDA! - ORIGINAL SONG BY MIRANDA SINGS

The fact that Miranda Sings has a song named after her is quite frankly a whole other level of amazingness. And anyone who says otherwise, is a big fibber. You're not a true star until you have a song named after you, soz! Just watch how Miranda owns this party.

CHECK IT OUT

jojo siwa

YouTube channels

Its JoJo Siwa - Official channel with dance videos from JoJo growing up, as well as sliming videos and a space to share her life updates with her fans.

JoJoVlogs - There just wasn't enough space on JoJo's first channel for all her vlogs, so she's got a second one! #winning

NAME: Joelle Joanie Siwa
DOB: 19/05/2003
Siblings: JoJo has a big brother called Jayden
Pets: BowBow, Coco and Lulu
Likes: Bows – she has over 700 of them!
Dislikes: People that sniffle too much with a cold. "Just blow your nose!"

f @itsjojosiwa
 @itsjojosiwa
 @itsjojosiwa

bio

3 of the best

Meet our all singing, all dancing YouTube star, JoJo Siwa! This gal started dance lessons as soon as she could walk and performed her first solo at the age of two. With dedication like that, it's no surprise that she's one of the biggest stars to come out of US reality TV show, Dance Moms. And now JoJo's joined Team Internet and has taken the world of YouTube by storm!

She's incredibly popular on social media generally but especially musically with her ItsJoJoSiwa channel gaining over 9 million fans. JoJo LOVES social media and interacting with her fans, which is probably part of the reason that she's gained so many loyal YouTube followers.

Her vlogs are super-energetic and chatty and involve fun things like prank calling her famous pals and doing the mannequin challenge, as well as sneaky peaks into her everyday life. We are well jel of her colour coordinated closet and gigantic shoe and bag collection. JoJo's weekly Q&A - which is called JoJo's Juice, involves JoJo pouring liquid over her head after she's answered your questions.

BOOMERANG

CHECK IT OUT

JoJo released her own song called BOOMERANG. We love it because it's all about positivity and standing up to haters. Go JoJo!

BOW BOW

They might've been banned at school, but JoJo's giant bows are the coolest! So cool in fact that she has a range at Claire's Accessories.

Teaching Miranda How To Twerk

CHECK IT OUT

CELEB PALS!

During Dance Moms, JoJo became great pals with Maddie Ziegler, who also has her own YouTube channel. Turn to page 74 to see why we think that Maddie's a YouTuber to watch in 2018.

Who Knows JoJo Better?!

CHECK IT OUT

#Say what?

We just can't figure out what's going on in the photos below! Got any ideas? Get creative and scribble down what YOU think your fave YouTubers are saying or dreaming about. We think the sillier the better!

dan TDM

Master of Minecraft!

Name: Daniel Middleton
DOB: 08/11/1991
Pets: Two pugs called Ellie and Darcie. Too cute!
Likes: The Incredibles movie
Dislikes: The dark

▶ YouTube channels

DanTDM – Tune in for all Dan's gaming and commentary videos.

MoreTDM – This channel is a chance to catch up with Dan's everyday life, as well as his pug shaped companions.

 @TheDiamondMinecart

 @dantdm

 @dantdm

DID YOU KNOW? Way back before Dan had launched his Minecart channel, he had a Pokemon vlog with the username PokemanDanLv45.

bio

Meet English YouTuber, Dan TDM, which stands for "Dan The Diamond Minecart". His massively successful gaming channel is focused on (you guessed it!) Minecraft, and his videos mostly involve him playing and commentating on all the action. Although Dan is most famous for his Minecraft vlogs, he's also made videos on Roblox and Nintendo's Tomodachi Life. His channel has gained over 14 million subscribers since joining in 2012!

3 of the best

I'm a Pikachu!

CHECK IT OUT

TOURING

His New York tour sold out in a matter of minutes! Tickets were said to be selling for up to 975 dollars each. Ouch!

When Minecraft pigs take over!

CHECK IT OUT

WINNING

Dan made it into the 2017 Guinness World Records Gamer's Edition with "Most views for a dedicated Minecraft video channel". The Diamond Minecart also nabbed the Nickelodeon Kids' Choice Award for "UK Favourite Tipster" two years running in 2015 and 2016.

Funny face swaps

CHECK IT OUT

BRAINY!

Dan went to university and has a degree in music production.

HE'S GOT HIS OWN BOOK!

5 favourite YouTube challenge videos of all time

YouTube is pretty much packed with dare and challenge videos, but some just look that bit more fun than all the rest!

1. THE HOUSEHOLD MAKEUP CHALLENGE WITH LOUISE

You know it's going to be good when Zoella and Louise Pentland are involved. For this challenge video, think shaving foam, flour and nutella. Ooh, and don't forget some maple syrup to really stick it all together. Results = a total LOL fest!

CHECK IT OUT

2. COUPLES GIANT JENGA CHALLENGE

Alfie, Zoe, Poppy and Sean get competitive and it's seriously one of the most intense games of Jenga we've ever seen!

CHECK IT OUT

FAMILY ICE BATH CHALLENGE

Fun-loving Alfie organised for 40 kilos of ice to be delivered to surprise his sister Poppy (we can think of kinder surprises TBH!), but it resulted in EVERYONE wanting a piece of the icy action, including Zoe! It makes us shiver just thinking about it.

CHECK IT OUT

FULL FACE USING ONLY KIDS MAKEUP CHALLENGE WITH JOJO SIWA

There's no holding back in this challenge – these guys really go all out. We think they look pretty fierce with their lip-gloss and glitter beards!

CHECK IT OUT

JOE SUGG'S ULTIMATE MANNEQUIN CHALLENGE

This is just awesome! They nail it. No more words – just watch it.

CHECK IT OUT

mark ferris

Why we can't get enough of Mark Ferris!

YouTube channels

@Mark Ferris – Mark's "wacky corner of YouTube" has 489k subscribers

DOB: 18/10/1990

Siblings: A sister called Amy – she's appeared on his channel

Pets: His adorable dog Teddi

~~Likes~~ **LOVES!:** One Direction

Dislikes: Clowns – he thinks they're scary and we kind of agree!

 @markyyferris

 @MarkFerris1990

bio

First things first, British YouTuber Mark Ferris is a total hoot and he's the guy that we all want to hang out with! He's well known for filming his Storytime vlogs, hauls, cooking (or trying to!), advice videos and Q&As – along with plenty of collabs with Team Zalfie, too.

Mark and Zoella are BFFs and their friendship is totally genuine. They met via YouTube but you can tell that they don't just post their collab videos to gain more subscribers – no, this friendship is the real deal. I think it's fair to say that this pair have all the laughs!

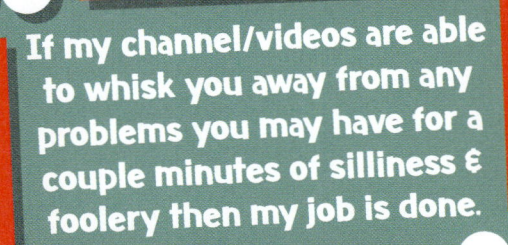

> " If my channel/videos are able to whisk you away from any problems you may have for a couple minutes of silliness & foolery then my job is done. "

FUN FACT ALERT!
Mark's appeared in some pretty big music videos.

The Wanted: We Own The Night

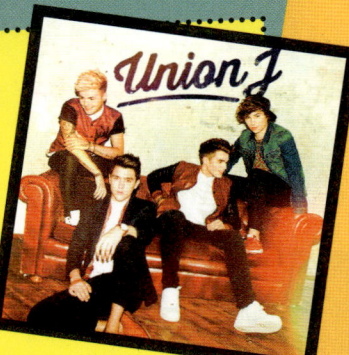

Union J: Beautiful Life

Ellie Goulding: Burn

3 of the best

British Guy Learns American Slang 
CHECK IT OUT

Two Truths, One Lie with Zoella 
CHECK IT OUT

Meet my new puppy 
CHECK IT OUT
Cuteness overload – we can't even deal!

The beauty edit

Are you always on the look out for inspiring beauty vloggers?

Well, my friends look no further! Here are 4 beauty vloggers that we're totally obsessed with right now.

Naomi Victoria

We all wish that Naomi could be our BFF. She's super chatty, friendly and so easy to listen to. Her channel covers everything from her morning routine, fashion hauls to DIY hair and beauty tutorials! It's like we're in the same room as her – plus she has oodles of cute ideas that are so on trend! We love her ombre pink hair tutorial.

Subscribers: 75, 359

Lewys

Proving that you don't have to be female to wear make-up, Lewys's channel is packed with hauls, tutorials, reviews and challenges. He's a self confessed lover of dogs, as well as high-end beauty products (a combo that we're all keen to get on board with!). What's more his brow game sure gives Cara Delevigne a run for her money! And his brows aren't the only thing Lewys has in common with Cara since he's become the face of Rimmel London's latest campaign. Oh-em-gee!

Subscribers: 163, 200

Fabulous Hannah

It's true, we've checked - Hannah really is fabulous! Best known for her fashion hauls, make-up challenges and GRWM (get ready with me vlogs), Hannah is down to earth, witty and watchable. Subscribing to her channel is like catching up with your bestie, while finding out about the hottest fashion and beauty trends! She has her own merchandise based on her life motto - "no rain, no flowers" too! Back in 2015, she even donated her long blond locks to the Little Princess Trust. Inspirational or what?

Subscribers: 238, 000

Kaushal Beauty

Super chatty with loads of handy tutorials that make new beauty trends seem accessible and achievable. She's got oodles of practical skincare and hair advice for everyday looks as well as special occasions. We especially love her Kylie Jenner inspired make-up tutorial, as well as her GRWM for an Indian wedding. It's hardly surprising that she's got a mahoosive fan base on Instagram with 619k followers.

Subscribers: 1,640,467

who is your vlogger BFF?

Follow the chart to see which famous YouTuber would be your ultimate bestie!

start

Do you love all things fashion and beauty?

- **YES** → I'm totally obsessed and I love keeping up to date with the latest trends.
- Not really. There are better ways to spend my time!

Do you love being the centre of attention?

- I prefer being around my friends or family because I'm super sociable. I get bored if I'm on my own too long!

NO

Do you enjoy spending time on your own?

- Yes – I like having my own space and I rarely get bored.

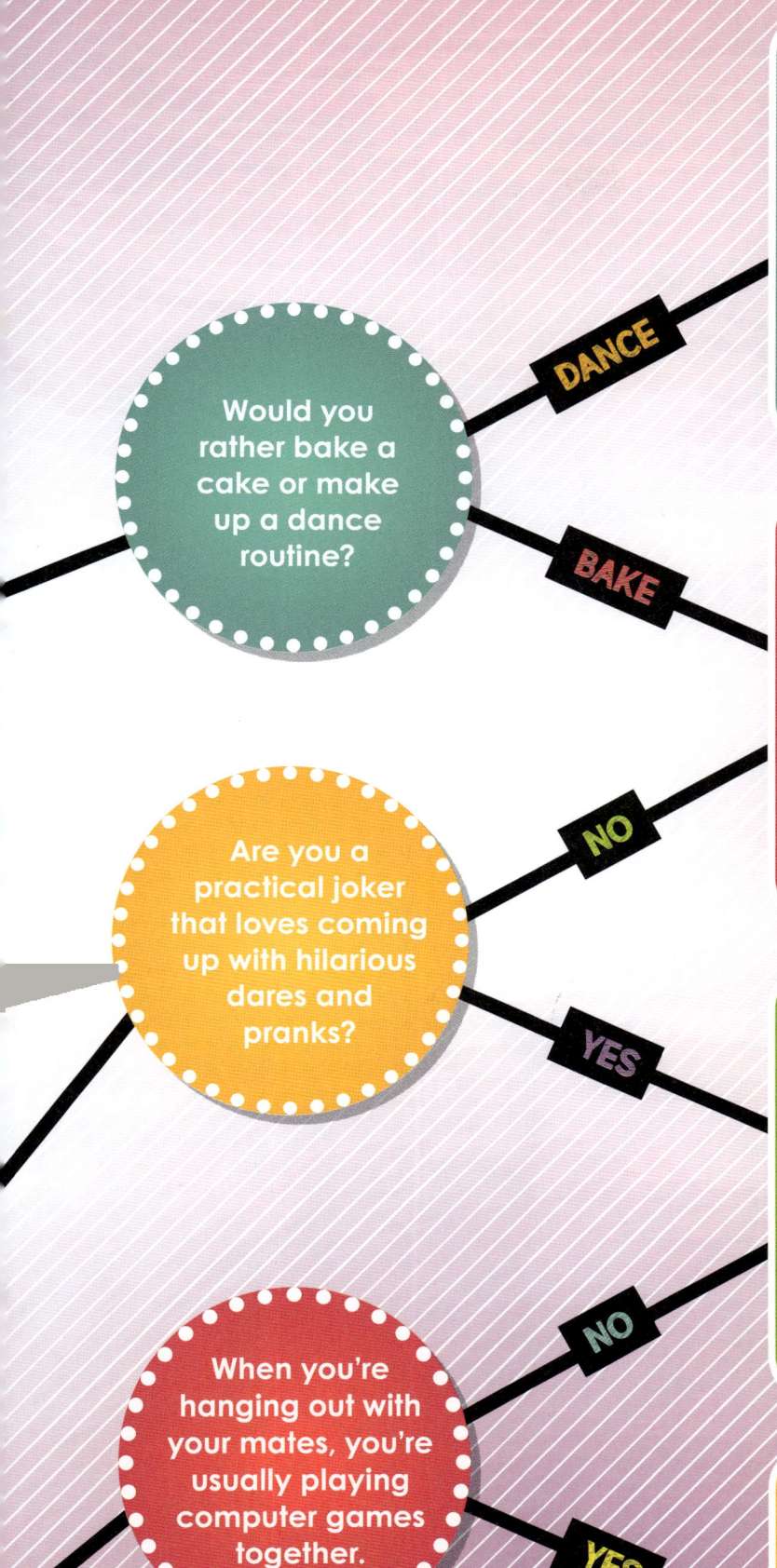

Would you rather bake a cake or make up a dance routine?

DANCE →

JOJO SIWA
Like JoJo, you've got your own unique signature style and you don't care what anyone else thinks. You're bold, colourful and fun with lots of energy and you both LOVE being the centre of attention.

BAKE →

TANYA BURR
You could swap beauty tips and you'd always have the coolest new look. When you're not doing makeovers on eachother, you'll be baking a masterpiece in the kitchen!

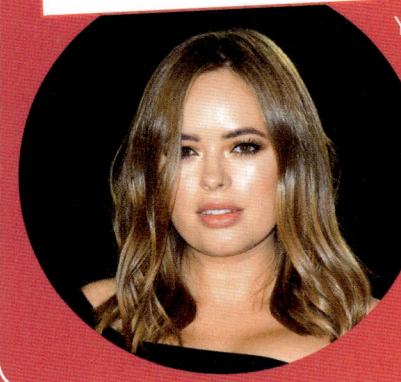

Are you a practical joker that loves coming up with hilarious dares and pranks?

NO →

YES →

THATCHER JOE
Your BFF is Joe Sugg. You two would always be up to mischief, whether you're pranking your pals or doing silly impressions of famous celebs, you would have tonnes of fun together.

When you're hanging out with your mates, you're usually playing computer games together.

NO →

YES →

DanTDM
You and DanTDM would be perfect pals! You could spend hours sharing your tips and tricks on your fave computer games. With so much in common, you'd never get bored of eachother's company.

43

ingrid nilsen

> "A place for curious minds and adventurous hearts"

DOB: 02/02/1989
Pets: A pooch called Tato
Likes: Reading!

- @heyingridnilsen
- @ingridnilsen
- @ingridnilsen

▶ YouTube channels

@Ingrid Nilsen - This is Ingrid's main channel.
@TheGridMonster - This is where you'll find Ingrid's vlogs and more!

bio

Californian YouTuber Ingrid was one of the first successful vloggers. Since launching her channel, she has gathered a huge following for her beauty tutorials, hauls and honest advice videos.

You may not know that Ingrid was once pretty shy and that's what inspired her to start vlogging in the first place. She saw her YouTube channel as a way to challenge herself – she'd always feared public speaking and thought this would be a great way to break that cycle.

Ingrid became super well known in 2015 when she posted her coming out video, Something I Want You To Know. This inspiring post has collected over 16 million views and it's had a big impact on many people.

Just when you thought Ingrid couldn't get any cooler, she also interviewed Obama in a live stream hosted at the White House in 2016. Most of us would be quaking in our boots at the very idea of talking to the president of the USA, but not Ingrid. She confidently took the issues most important to her and her subscribers to the president. Representing #TeamInternet and doing them proud!

FUN FACT
Ingrid is ambidextrous which means that she's both right and left handed. Cool, eh?

TOP ACHIEVEMENTS
At the 2014 Teen Choice Awards, Ingrid was nominated for Choice Web Star: Fashion/Beauty. That same year, she won the Best Beauty Program at the Streamy Awards.

3 of the best

Live Spring Haul!
CHECK IT OUT

My Shoe Collection
CHECK IT OUT

March Faves! Makeup, Fashion, Books + More!
CHECK IT OUT

5 awesome things we learned from Vsauce

We wish we could absorb all the facts from the collective brains of Michael, Kevin and Jake. Probs not gonna happen, but these facts will be a good start!

1. DINOSAUR SCIENCE! feat. Chris Pratt and Jack Horner

Everyone knows that dinosaurs went extinct, duh! But DID they though? Get your brain around this fascinating Dinosaur Science video before you make your mind up. You might be surprised.

CHECK IT OUT

2. ULTIMATE ROOM MAKEOVER PRANK

You've dropped your sandwich on the floor, again! But is the five-second rule a scientific fact? Well, apparently not! Even 5 seconds on the floor is long enough to transfer bacteria to our food. Hmmm, so maybe we shouldn't eat our food off the floor no matter how short a time it's down there. Check it out to learn more.

CHECK IT OUT

3 WE ARE ALL RELATED

We are all related. Which doesn't sound all that shocking at first, but what got us was the fact that we're much more closely related than you might assume. "Scientifically speaking, geneticists tell us that every single person on earth is at the least 50th cousins with everybody else on earth." It's a lot to take in, so we'll hand you over to the experts.

CHECK IT OUT

4 IS IT OKAY TO TOUCH MARS?

We're 0.00000000000000001% martian. Our bodies are likely to contain billions of atoms from Mars that arrived on earth in the last 1,000 years. Don't believe us? Check out this video.

CHECK IT OUT

5 TALKING WITH ATTENBOROUGH

One of our favourite moments of Vsauce's videos was when he talks with Sir David Attenborough! They discuss the responsibility that our generation has to record nature around us with technology as it becomes available (Team Internet, that means you!). Listen in to hear about the importance of telling a story and keeping a record for future generations to better understand our planet and better survive.

CHECK IT OUT

guess who?

"Teehee"

Are you a total know-it-all when it comes to all things YouTuber? Put your knowledge to the test and see if you know which famous Vlogger said the words below. Let's do this thing.

"I didn't choose the Sugg life, the Sugg life chose me."

"Peace out, enjoy life and live the adventure!"

"I'll be a YouTuber for as long as I love it."

"Don't cry, craft!"

Miranda Sings

Vsauce

Ryan Higa

Dan & Phil

48

"Aloha, sprinklerinos!"

"Haters back off!"

"No rain, no flowers"

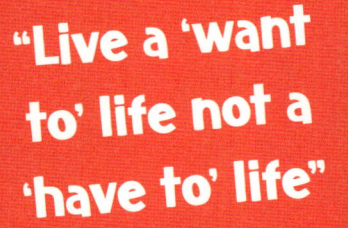

"Live a 'want to' life not a 'have to' life"

"And as always, thanks for watching."

Now, turn to page 77 to check your answers!

Fun for Louis

Zoella

Joe Sugg

Sprinkle of Glitter

Tyler Oakley

Fabulous Hannah

my YouTube set

Will you take inspo from Zoella and vlog from your room? Doodle your fave interiors here.

Remember, you can go all out with your design - FYI there's no budget in a dream...

Grab your brightest pens to design your dream set! Remember this will be the backdrop to most of your vlogs, so be sure to fill it with the styles, colours and things that best represent YOU.

Why not add cool features like a 'on air' light to let your family know when you're recording?

my YouTube channel

You've designed an awesome set, now it's time to brainstorm ideas for the awesome content you'll create to fill your channel with!

My YouTube name will be...

Ideas for my first video...

I'd like these people to feature in my videos...

I will collaborate with...

Before you begin, have a think about the vlogs you watch the most and the channels that you just wish existed.

Tags I'll use...

My vlog will be ALL ABOUT....

I will take inspiration from...

F2 freestylers

Billy Wingrove and Jeremy Lynch

f @TheF2Freestylers
📷 @thef2
🐦 @TheF2

▶ YouTube channels

F2Freestylers – Ultimate Soccer Skills Channel with match-play tutorials, entertainment and all the banter!

bio

The F2Freestylers is the Ultimate Soccer Skills Channel and is made up of Billy Wingrove & Jeremy Lynch. Their channel, which has over 5 million subscribers and is packed with match-play tutorials, live performances, lots of pranks and even guest appearances.

About Billy
Billy made it to the semi-final of the Nike freestyle competition in London in 2003, beating almost 6,000 others. He's made television appearances on the likes of Nickelodeon, BBC and Sky Sports, while also playing traditional football for clubs like Enfield FC.

About Jeremy
You might not have heard that Jeremy made it all the way to the finals as a contestant on Britain's Got Talent in 2008! And if that wasn't enough, Jeremy has also made videos with some of the world's biggest football stars, including Cristiano Ronaldo and Nani.

SUCH RASCALS!
They've got their own clothing line, Rascal Clothing. #BeRascal

FOR ANY BUDDING FOOTBALLERS OUT THERE...
These uber talented fellas also have a book that might just be right up your street! It's called **F2 World of Football: How to Play Like a Pro**

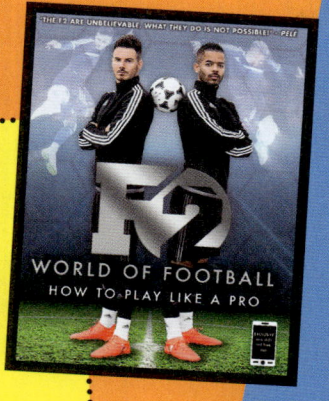

FUN FACT! Billy appeared with Wayne Rooney in a promotion for Coca-Cola.

3 of the best

CELEBRATIONS ft. LOGAN PAUL
CHECK IT OUT

Luis Suarez teaches us how to always score 1V1 vs goalkeeper
CHECK IT OUT

VIRAL FOOTBALL
CHECK IT OUT

dan and phil

Let's catch up with delightful duo, Dan and Phil

f @DanAndPhilGAMES

🐦 @DanAndPhilGAMES

▶ YouTube channels

DanAndPhilGAMES – 2,775,895 subscribers
Let's play, challenges and reviews – along with all the general Dan and Phil banter that you could wish for.

bio

These guys have made awkwardness cool and that's why we love them so. At the very core of what they do, Dan and Phil believe that it's okay to be weird – more than okay, they celebrate it! Since meeting online through their shared passion for gaming, these lads have continued to pave the way for YouTubers around the world.

As you probably already know, these chaps were the first vloggers to be given their own Radio 1 show. And we're pleased to report that their incredible success is still on the up, with no sign of slowing down! Phil Lester won creator of the year at the BONCAS (British Online Creator Awards). What's more, the pair also won best collaboration, too! They're on a roll.

3 of the best

The making of The Amazing Book is not on Fire

CHECK IT OUT

IMPRESSIVE!

At Summer in the City 2015 (an annual event dedicated to YouTube content creators and users) their channel was announced as the fastest growing in YouTube history. Wow!

Dan and Phil play Just Dance

CHECK IT OUT

THEY HAVE A BOOK, TOO!

Their book, The Amazing Book Is Not On Fire, was number one in the UK charts and a New York bestseller.

MORE MOVIE APPEARANCES!

Dan and Phil are the voices of two gorilla princes in Disney's The Lion Guard. In the animated series, Dan plays Majinuni, and Phil voices Hafifu, two fancy gorillas who've even got Dan and Phil's sweeping side fringes that we all know and love.

THE BEST GAME EVER MADE:

CHECK IT OUT

THE 7 SECOND CHALLENGE

STOP! Do not read any further until you have a pen and a stopwatch. It's time to recreate Dan and Phil's infamous 7 Second Challenge right here, right now!

When you're ready, flip your annual upside down to reveal the first topic and start writing! You must write the first things you think of for each topic. And be quick about it… 7 seconds for each topic isn't long. Have fun!

Loaf

Make-up

Farm

Sleep

Toad

Jelly

now try your own in these blank spaces and try them out on your pals

WHAT TYPE OF YouTuber ARE YOU?

Do you prefer Tanya Burr or PewDiePie? Answer the questions below to discover what type of vlogger you should be!

1. Your perfect weekend would involve...
a) Having my friend over to play with all my Shopkins.
b) Being outdoors and playing a sport of any kind.
c) Doing makeovers on my besties!
d) Being first in line for a new game going on sale.

2. You're most likely to spend your pocket money on...
a) Toys! Shopkins, Pokemon... I collect everything!
b) Water balloons or footballs!
c) Make-up or new clothes.
d) A new game for my xbox

3. In your friendship group you are the...
a) Leader – I'm always the first to plan fun things to do, or organise a game to play.
b) Clown – I love pulling pranks to make people laugh!
c) Listener – I am the one people go to for advice.
d) I just have one best friend, as big groups intimidate me.

4. The word that best describes you is...
a) Fun – I don't take life too seriously.
b) Daring
c) Trendy – I love staying up to date with the latest fashion styles.
d) Geeky

5. Your favourite subject at school is...
a) I don't really have one...
b) Games or P.E. – sport is my passion.
c) Art – I love being creative.
d) Maths – I love problem solving!

Mostly A's: Toy Vlogger
You should be a Toy Vlogger. When it comes to the latest toy trends, you're the top dog and you know what'll be a bestseller. You are full of fun and love collecting all the latest toys, plus you know your Shopkins from your Shoppies and love nothing more than spending time with your pals and talking about the latest toys to collect.

Mostly B's: Sport and dares
You should be a Sports Vlogger! You're energetic, daring and determined. Your idea of heaven would be spent in your garden or the local park with your mates, competing in exciting sporty challenges! You love coming up with funny dares and you're not embarrassed when it comes to making a fool out of yourself. Fair play, you'd be perfect.

6 Your fave vlogger is...

a) Toys AndMe   **b)** W2S   **c)** Sprinkle of Glitter   **d)** DanTDM

7 You're most likely to be told off for...

a) Having a messy bedroom. I collect everything!
b) Being immature!
c) Taking ages to get ready and making everyone late.
d) Spending too much time in my room – even when the weather is nice outdoors.

8 The best thing about going on holiday (or just not being at school!) is...

a) Playing tonnes of board games with my pals
b) Having epic water fights and just being outdoors all the time.
c) Getting to show off my new holiday wardrobe!
d) More time to reach the next level on the game I'm playing

9 If you could choose to be an animal, you would be a...

a) Dolphin – sociable and playful!
b) Cheetah – full of energy
c) Horse – graceful and loves being centre of attention.
d) Penguin – problem solving pro and determined

10 It's sports day and your first thought is...

a) I'll do the egg and spoon race for a laugh.
b) I need to start training, I've got to win!
c) My gym kit needs an update. Time for a shopping trip!
d) How can I get out of it? Sports day is the worst.

Mostly C's: Beauty Vlogger

You should be a Beauty Vlogger. You're a true fashionista and you're ALWAYS in the know when it comes to the best beauty brands and hair 'dos and don'ts! You're not afraid to experiment with a bold new look and people admire your creative approach to fashion. People would be sure to tune in to hear your beauty tips and tricks!

Mostly D's: Gaming

You should be a Gaming Vlogger. You're a problem solver and fast thinker and you're always first to get your hands on the latest game. What's more, you never give up and are always first to make it through the next level, no matter how hard it is. Move over, DanTDM, cause there's a new gamer in town!

TOP picks

Let's take a moment to marvel at the YouTubers who are totally slaying it in their category!

TRAVEL

Fun for Louis
1,905,493 subscribers.

Louis Cole is a vlogger that gets to travel the world for a living and share every step of his adventure with his fans via YouTube – I mean, who doesn't wish they were Louis?! He's experienced things most of us would only ever dream of, from skydiving to standing on the rim of an active volcano, to visiting Niagra Falls and even camel surfing (is that a real thing?). We could literally talk about his escapades for days, but we'll let you subscribe to his channel instead. Next up for this go-getter is to make a feature length travel documentary with his friend Juan-Peter (JP). Watch this space...

BAKING

Cupcake Jemma
964,786 subscribers.

Meet the queen of all things baking, Cupcake Jemma. If you need a jaw-dropping, head-turning bake or 10, Jemma is your gal. Jamie Oliver invited Jemma to launch her YouTube channel on his food network, Food Tube and her following has built and built from there. Subscribe to her incredible channel for rainbow polka dot swiss-rolls, unicorn cakes and more. You'll also get behind the scenes action at the incredible Crumbs and Doilies Cupcakes – a bakery of which she is founder and owner.

PRANKS Caspar Lee

YouTube sensation Caspar Lee was brought up in South Africa but now lives in London. He's the King of YouTube pranks and is always one step ahead with the next trick up his sleeve. His most-viewed video is called "Girlfriend pranks my roommate". If his channel wasn't exciting enough already, Caspar's also had plenty of celebs on board, including Ed Sheeran. To top it all off, he's also been in two movies – "Spud 3" and the SpongeBob Movie "Sponge Out of Water."

7,154,936 subscribers.

COMEDY

Miranda Sings
7,675,487 subscribers.

Miranda Sings is a fictional character played by American comedian, Colleen Ballinger, and she's hands-down the wackiest red lipstick-wearing vlogger that the US has to offer. Miranda's hilarious content is fun, unique and so unbelievably watchable! If you're looking for a YouTuber who gives themselves a full face of fake nails, or posts an "All of Beauty and the Best in 1 minute" video (you've got to see it to believe it…), then here's your woman. She's toured all over the world for her "mirfandas" (that's what she calls her fans!).

RAPPER, COMEDIAN AND ACTOR

KSI
KSI, real name Olajide Olatunji, is an English YouTube personality and social media phenomenon at the top of his game RN. You're likely to know him for his iconic Sax Guy video, which involves KSI in a snazzy gold onesie – what's not to love? But he's also famous for FIFA, football, music and comedy content. Like many other successful YouTubers, KSI has done his bit for charity and was even the face of Sport Relief Online in 2014.

16,071,322 subscribers.

Who's your fave vlogger of all time? They could be somebody in this annual, or somebody completely different. Write yours in the space provided.

The best vlogger is…………
Joe Sugg & Caspar lee & Jack Maynard & Roman Atwood

I love them because…………
Because they are all funny and amazing and entertaining and I just love them all.

bestseller

All good YouTubers bring out their own book! Whether you like it or loathe it, this is just how it goes. Use the grid below to reveal what your first bestseller would be

First, find the month that you were born in:

- **January:** Famous
- **February:** Dream
- **March:** Star
- **April:** Fabulous
- **May:** Unstoppable
- **June:** Secret
- **July:** Magnificent
- **August:** Destination
- **September:** All-star
- **October:** Un-stoppable
- **November:** Tap
- **December:** Favourite

Now, choose the first pet you ever had:

- **Cat:** Online
- **Dog:** Vlogger
- **Rabbit:** Chat
- **Guinea pig:** Me
- **Hamster:** Collection
- **Gerbil:** Right Now
- **Other:** Forever
- **None:** Feature

Now, put the two words together to find the title for your first book! For example, if you were born in August and your first pet was a cat, your book would be called Destination Online.

TIME TO design YOUR BOOK!

Now it's time to come up with a cool design for the cover of your book! Will you use photographs, stencils, or even design your own character? Be creative and make sure the cover is as awesome as the title!

#SPOT and FIND

Having an adorable ball of fluff to sit with you while you vlog all day long is essential. Beady eyes at the ready, folks! It's your job to find all the YouTuber pets in the picture.

Martha (Jim and Tanya sausage dog)

Maliboo (Maddie Ziegler's dog)

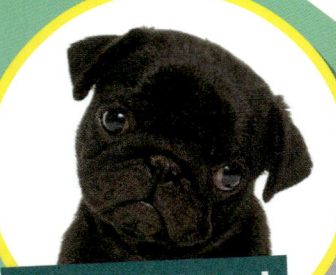

Nala (Zoella and Alfie's pug)

Popcorn (Caspar Lee's dog)

Tato (Ingrid Nilsen's pomeranion)

Rocket and Zula (Sprinkle of Glitter's cats)

Teddi (Mark Ferris' dog)

Slippy (PewDiePie's toad)

Check your anwers on **page 76**

14 times that youtubers words inspired us!

We wish that we were this wise! Sometimes our favourite vloggers seem to be the only ones talking any sense around here. With their words of wisdom and advice aplenty – they sure are good eggs.

Don't worry about things that haven't happened yet. Treat everyday as an adventure!

Confidence is all about finding yourself and being happy with yourself!

Sometimes you have to face your fears to realise that they aren't actually real.

Not all of life is beautiful and amazing but you can learn to understand the meaning behind it…

Ingrid Nilsen

You should never strive for perfection because it doesn't exist and that's never going to make you feel happy. Embrace who you are – don't follow!

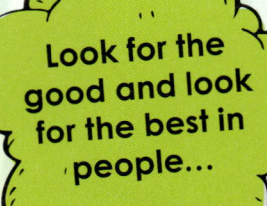

Look for the good and look for the best in people…

68

Talk to yourself like you are your own best friend. Your best friend is going to point out your best things!

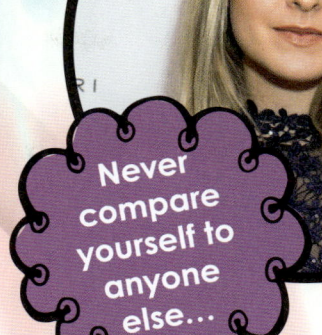

Never compare yourself to anyone else...

You've got to not put pressure on yourself to make friends. That's when you stop being who you are just to please other people.

Surround yourself with people who are the ketchup to your french fries - they make you a better version of yourself. Yes french fries are amazing on their own, but combined with ketchup they are a force. Spend time with people who bring out your true flavours, but don't overpower you.

You are an independent mind in this universe that can do everything and anything you have ever dreamed of.

Be yourself. Don't worry about what other people are thinking of you, because they're probably feeling the same kind of scared, horrible feelings that everyone does.

Connor Franta

I was taught that being myself was not only okay, but encouraged - and by being unapologetically yourself, you thrive and inspire others to thrive.

I refuse to hope things will get better in the future when I have complete control over making them the best possible right here and now.

THE ULTIMATE vlogger QUIZ

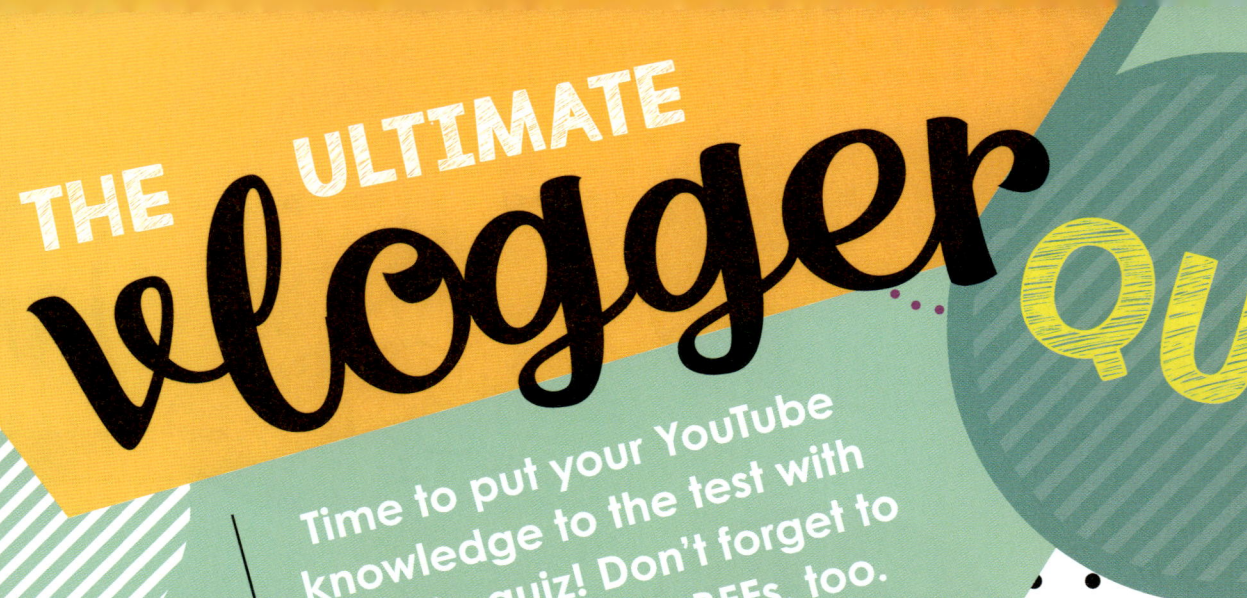

Time to put your YouTube knowledge to the test with our epic quiz! Don't forget to try it out on your BFFs, too.

1 JoJo Siwa has a book out called JoJo's Guide to the Sweet Life, true or false?

2 Who's cute pooch is this?

3 What's the name of Alfie Deyes' sister?

4 Which vlogging duo are the voices of two gorilla princes in Disney's The Lion Guard?

5 True or false, Tyler Oakley has his own glasses range?

6 Can you name all the YouTubers in this mixed up pic?

7 Who calls their fans "Sugglets?"

8 Which YouTuber has their own range of hair bows at Claire's Accessories?

9 Which YouTuber won creator of the year at the BONCAs in 2016, Dan Howell or Phil Lester?

10 Ingrid Nilsen interviewed Barack Obama, true or false?

11 What movie sequel did a handful of our vlogger pals feature in – Love Actually or The Holiday?

12 Who's older, Zoe or Alfie?

13 What does the GRWM tag stand for?

14 Which vlogger celebrated their subscriber milestone by getting a play button tattoo on their ankle?

....

15 Who's got a YouTube channel called Famtastic?

....

16 Miranda Sings is famous for her iconic red lipstick, true or false?

....

17 Which drive through did Tiana from Toys AndMe go to in her toy car?

....

18 Which vlogger was mentioned on Coronation Street?

....

19 Who voiced a seagull in Spongebob: Sponge Out Of Water?

....

20 Which YouTube couple make up Janya?

....

21 "The Pointless Book" is the title of which vlogger's book?

....

22 What has Jim Chapman got a degree in?

....

23 Who has a TV show called Haters Back Off, Miranda Sings or Zoella?

24 What did Oli White play competitively whilst at school?

a) badminton
b) rounders
c) chess
d) tennis

25 What nationality is PewDiePie – Swedish or Welsh?

26 Name these two YouTubers in these blurred photographs.

27 Tanya Burr's first book was called "Love, Tanya" - true or false?

28 Which YouTubers featured together on Ant and Dec's Saturday Night Takeaway?

Check your answers on **page 76-77** because it's time to count up your scores!

0-5 LOL! I think you should re-read this annual!!!

6-10 There is room for improvement...

11-15 Great effort!

16-20 You sure know your stuff.

21-25 Oh-em-gee! We're bowled over.

26+ You're a TOTAL PRO!

73

Ones to Watch

Who wants some more YouTube talent to subscribe to? Everyone – thought so! These are a handful of the vloggers that we're most excited about RN!

Lucy Moon

Lucy's a cool British YouTuber who's a feminist, and she's all about good music and positivity. She posts weekly vlogs on topics including advice, make-up, and baking with her besties. One of our favourites is the way that she discusses what it's like to be considered a role model online. She's smart, honest and downright interesting and she already has 227 thousand subscribers.

Jazmyn Bieber

Yep, that's right - Justin Bieber's little sister has her own YouTube channel and we predict BIG things! Within the first few months of launching with her "Official Trailer" Jazmyn picked up over 2 million views. We can't wait to find out what this mini-Bieber wants to share with the world.

Brendan Jordan

Brendan Jordan is an American YouTuber who identifies as trans and his content is already having a huge impact. His vlog is all about advice, fashion and make-up and he's not afraid to open up or push boundaries. And in doing so, he's inspired many people from the LGBTQ+ community. He's also caught the eye of celebrities including Lady Gaga and Miley Cyrus.

Maddie Ziegler

Maddie is a talented dancer, actress and model best known for being on Dance Moms (along with her mate, JoJo Siwa). She's also starred in a number of Sia's famous music videos and even toured with her! But we're most excited about her brand new YouTube channel where she's started sharing beauty tips and fun challenges. She's not posted much yet, but we're eagerly awaiting her next post!

answers

20-21 Spot the difference

10-11 Wordsearch

48-49 Guess Who?

"Haters back off!"
Miranda Sings

"Teehee"
Ryan Higa

"And as always, thanks for watching."
Vsauce

"Don't cry, craft!"
Dan and Phil

"Aloha, sprinklerinos!"
Sprinkle of Glitter

"Live a 'want to' life not a 'have to' life
Zoella

"No rain, no flowers"
Fabulous Hannah

"I didn't choose the Sugg life, the Sugg life chose me."
Joe Sugg

"I'll be a YouTuber for as long as I love it."
Tyler Oakley

"Peace out, enjoy life and live the adventure!"
Fun for Louis

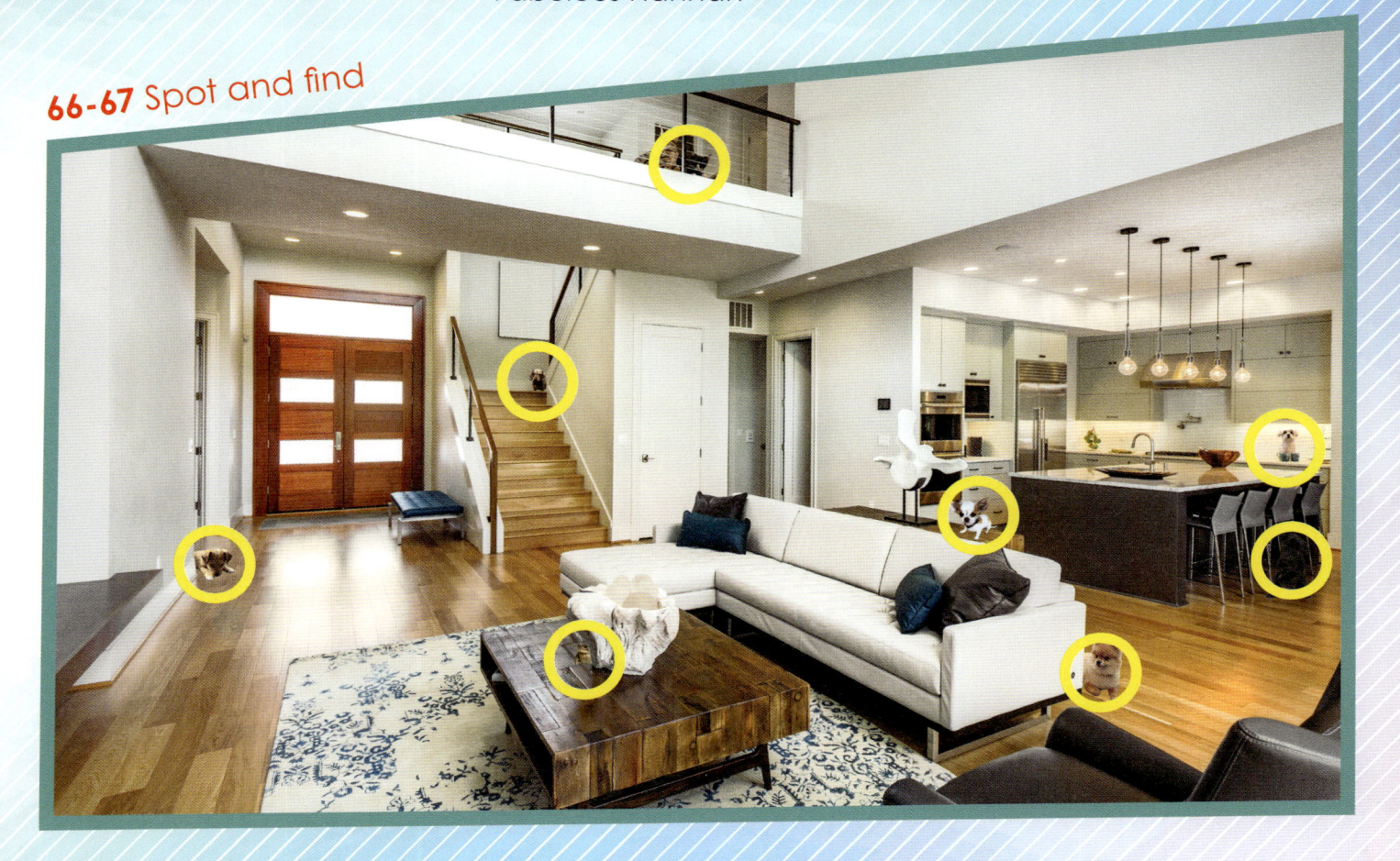

66-67 Spot and find

70-73 The Ultimate Vlogger Quiz

1. true
2. Ingrid Nilsen's
3. Poppy
4. Dan and Phil
5. True
6. Alfie Deyes, Fleur De Force, Sprinkle of Glitter
7. Joe Sugg
8. JoJo Siwa
9. Phil Lester
10. true
11. Love Actually
12. Zoe
13. Get Ready With Me
14. Caspar Lee
15. Toys AndMe – Tiana
16. True
17. McDonald's
18. Zoella
19. Caspar Lee
20. Tanya Burr and Jim Chapman
21. Alfie Deyes
22. Psychology
23. Miranda Sings
24. badminton
25. Swedish
26. Oli White and Mark Ferris
27. True
28. Marcus Butler and Alfie Deyes

PICTURE CREDITS

Cover:

Zoella - Matt Alexander/PA Archive/PA Vsauce - John Phillips/PA Archive/PA Thatcher Joe - David Jensen/EMPICS Entertainment, Alfie Deyes - Doug Peters/EMPICS Entertainment, Ingrid Nilsen - Sipa USA/SIPA USA/PA Images, JoJo Siwa - © Faye Sadou/AdMedia via ZUMA Wire, Toys AndMe - John Nguyen/PA Archive/PA Images

Back cover:

Laura Lean/PA Archive/PA Images, David Jensen/EMPICS Entertainment, Matt Crossick/PA Archive/PA Images, Van Tine Dennis/ABACA/ABACA/PA Images

Content:

4-5: Dominic Lipinski/PA Archive/PA Images, Matt Crossick/PA Archive/PA Images, Admedia, Inc/SIPA USA/PA Images

6-7: Matt Alexander/PA Archive/PA Images, David Jensen/EMPICS Entertainment, Jonas Ekstrmer/TT/TT News Agency/Press Association Images, John Phillips/PA Archive/PA Images, Dominic Lipinski/PA Archive/PA Images, Ian West/PA Wire/PA Images

8-9: Doug Peters/EMPICS Entertainment, Jonathan Hordle/REX/Shutterstock

12-13: AJM/EMPICS Entertainment, Ian West/PA Archive/PA Images

18-19: John Nguyen/PA Archive/PA Images

20-21: Geoff Caddick/PA Archive/PA Images, Sipa USA/SIPA USA/PA Images

22-23: SEE LI/NEWZULU/PA Images, James M Warren/Silverhub/REX/Shutterstock

24-25: Faye Sadou/Admedia/Zuma Press/PA Images

30-31: John Salangsang/SIPA USA/PA Images, Admedia, Inc/SIPA USA/PA Images

32-33: Yui Mok/PA Archive/PA Images, Geoff Caddick/PA Archive/PA Images

42-43: Ian West/PA Wire, © Dave Longendyke/Globe Photos via ZUMA Wire

44-45: Anthony Behar/SIPA USA/PA Images

48-49: LuMarPhoto/AFF/PA Images, David Jensen/EMPICS Entertainment, Matt Crossick/PA Archive/PA Images, © AdMedia via ZUMA Wire

56-57: Matt Crossick/PA Archive/PA Images

58-59: Ian West/PA Wire

68-69: David Jensen/EMPICS Entertainment, Ian West/PA Wire, © Tony Lowe/Globe Photos via ZUMA Wire, Matt Crossick/PA Archive/PA Images, © Birdie Thompson/AdMedia via ZUMA Wire, Van Tine Dennis/ABACA/ABACA/PA Images

70-73: Matt Crossick/ EMPICS Entertainment, RE/Westcom/Starmax/PA Images, Matt Crossick/PA Archive/PA Images

74-75: © Tony Lowe/Globe Photos via ZUMA Wire, © Faye Sadou/AdMedia via ZUMA Wire

76-77: Geoff Caddick/PA Archive/PA Images, Sipa USA/SIPA USA/PA Images